D1003827

To Fly without Hurry

This book made possible through the *Richard Walser and Bernice Kelly Harris Fund* of the Hanes Charitable Lead Trust

Library of Congress Cataloging-in-Publication Data

Wilson, Emily Herring/to fly without hurry/
Emily Herring Wilson—Laurinburg, NC/St. Andrews College Press
I. Wilson, Emily Herring II. Title

St. Andrews College Press
1700 Dogwood Mile
Laurinburg, NC 28352

www.sapc.edu/sapress.html

For Melinda
with Julie's love —
And mine —
Emily

To Fly without Hurry

Poems
by

Emily Herring Wilson

Emily Bay Wilson

St. Andrews College Press
Laurinburg, North Carolina
2001

For longing

Acknowledgments

Some of these poems were published many years ago in earlier chapbooks, now long since fallen into history. Some of them have found their way into journals that I cannot remember and that cannot remember me, though I wish to thank all those editors (some friends) who encouraged me at once with their acceptances. The great teacher in my life has been A.R. Ammons. More recently, one of his students at Cornell, Amy Whitney, has taught me. Again, Elizabeth Phillips is a generous reader. I wish to thank LeAnne Howe for teaching me to see ghosts. My literary influences in these poems are Toni Morrison's novel *Beloved*, A.R. Ammons' poem "For Harold Bloom," Willa Cather's novel *Death Comes for the Archbishop*, Elizabeth Bishop's poem "Sestina," and *The Book of Common Prayer*. The new poems were written in celebration of my sixtieth year to heaven and in gratitude to St. Andrews College Press.

E.H.W.
May 1, 2000

The House of History
for Seth ("Me? Me?")

Please, Beloved, give up haunting our house.
I leave the doors unlocked,
Stitch soft white curtains.
All morning small birds feed
From my hands. I have asked for forgiveness.
Let our love overcome our fears.
Come, sit with me?
Take up these poems

Waiting for you.

Finding Help

I run to hide,
Crashing through underbrush,
Looking for some deep hole
Or the back of a creek bank,

Never an open field, never that.
I listen, and all around
Voices like my voice
Names like mine cry out.

We leave signs
Along the way. Come,
There is a way in.

Banking

When you have stayed with the fire
Until it dies, and you shiver
And go up to bed, your old charred
Sticks wobbly with loss,
Sleep will come. I know that.
I want to say to you,
Listen for the silence breaking.
The ashes will sputter.
The untended will attend.

Staying Put

If you stay where you are
I can find in
You permanence

So that when I am lost
Calling out can anyone help
You'll turn on the light

And bring me home.

Balancing on Stones

Perhaps the light bending
  in the wheat
Or the pale undersides of
  summer leaves
Filled up the old silences
  between us.
We found our way easy,
  across small streams,
Walking in field daisies,
  naming birds.

Then we came to the place
  no human talk
Makes sound without pushing
  beyond the limits
To where pain lies, dark
  as the creek banks,
Pushing from a darker source,
  washing upon us,
Adrift, frightened, quick

Balancing on stones.

A Private Life

All night she hears the crashing of branches,
The click of ice, the winter wind. Dark sounds.

She reads to keep her mind busy, old letters
Again, once more. Not a time to phone or visit.

Those she most loved, dead. The world she knew,
Gone. She checks Mother's day book: "Cold rain."

She looks up, can she have heard the postman?
Of course not, be sensible. Shh. Wait for the light.

The Letter-Writing

Her body leans to the table, touching
Words. In the sleeping house, hers
Is the only motion except the fire's.

She tosses her life
To the flames and studies
The pieces. The smoke sighs.

Each day, she rises to complete the letter.
The distance draws her. She fills her cup,
The taste is good.

By daylight, she puts away, closes up.
Her face is sweet. She must go
To the sleepers, waking hungry.

When he leaves for work, he'll walk
In the yard, a happy man, and smell
The hickory burning, and like the smell.

Inside, she stirs the fire.

Birthday

A long avenue of houses
An alley of boiling washpots
And a narrow yard

Where sun strikes a match
To the crepe myrtle tree
And my body bursts into bloom.

Mother Voices

Mother reads to me in my sick bed.
My world's the upstairs room.
I'm propped on pillows, given strength
Through a bent straw for my own good.

My sister cannot come to see me.
She sends me letters in a divided house.
Outside, the crepe myrtle blooms
With children's shouts: come to the window.
I shut them out; the doctor shut me in.

My mother reads to me, we are alone.
She holds the book in one hand
And holds me with the other.
I don't want to go to sleep.
Go on, go on, I say, and the voice
Goes on. The lamp's shaded with
A newspaper for my eyes.

The next morning I must have been
Asleep, not dead. My doll hit the floor
And broke her head.
Mother opens Monday's present
And takes away the doll in pieces.

Now I am sick again, an adult who
Cries No! but my mother has come
To stay with me. I don't know
What I want—a glass of water
And a shaded lamp won't do.

The telephone rings, and I won't
Answer. Neighbors come to the door.
My mother walks back and forth.
So I say, read to me, and she

Reads, and her voice sounds
Scared, like a child's. I'm going to be
Okay, I say, don't worry.
Look out the window.

What I Overheard When I was a Child and What I Made Up

She folded her fur coat and left it on the bank,
Took off one black shoe, then the other, and last,
Took off her rings and placed them on a rock.
Then she walked straight into the cold river.

From the bridge where he was fishing,
A man watched her go down.
I think she drowned.

Boundaries

"The boundary between sea and land is the most fleeting
and transitory feature on the earth."

—Rachel Carson, *The Sea Around Us*

The ocean rises,
Buries boats
Ribs
Fish bones.

An old woman dreams
She swims with porpoises,
Shining half-moons.

An old man dreams she's sun-
Ripe fruit,
Sweet basil, and mint.

"The ocean is overfull.
It is spilling over
The rim of its basins."

He reaches for her,
But she moves,
Lifted by waves.

For the Last Time, Then Once More

The day you see the wrinkled hand
Reaching for something familiar—
A book, a mirror, a child—
And realize the hand is yours

Is a day you will remember longer
Than any birthday. Late at night
You are awake to count each year,
Asking for one more chance to feel
Your heart pounding with desire.

This gray day

This gray day
Wants change
For the crinkled leaves
To unfold
To fly up and stick
To the thin high branches
For the solitary bird
To settle
And renew his song
And for the January jasmine
To let go
With raucous yellow laughter.

What We Make of What We See

Iconography in a Rural Landscape

A woman saw God smile in a Carolina tobacco field
Somewhere between Richlands and Jacksonville.
When she told it at home, Uncle Alton laughed.
Said she's most likely seen her first double rainbow.

Red Peppers in a Black Bowl

The poet picks words
Feels the humps of some
The lengths of others
But finishes
Hungry
Nothing
Having satisfied
The taste
She sees.

Time's Anatomy

I lost the front porch
Of my Georgia childhood,
My dog run over by the bus,
My tablet left out in the rain,

Mr. Clark sun-bathing naked
On the roof, Miss Rochelle
Babying her only boy, grown,
Miss Banner, driving.

I go looking for them now
Riding through this small
Town, near dark, when every
Door closes and shades are drawn

And in the back room around
A table everyone belongs
And every house reminds me
Of my own.

Splitting Wood

The woodsman's wedge
Centers the log.
He lifts his sledge
Against November.
He knows
What the hammer knows.

The log I couldn't roll
Splits evenly.
Next year
Its cold beauty will burn.

I lift a page, looking
For a center
To mark.
My heart beats
Like a woodsman's:
My hands are hot.

O Careless Love

Wind and rain whip the trees. Dogwood, maple, sycamore,
Poplar, all bare. Stubborn oak gives up the ghost. Then

Comes a rush of news, dressed in blackcaps, tufts, reds and
Greens, bright beaks. Jittery, skittery wings. And all talking

At once: can you believe this weather? It feels like summer.
Oh, yes, pass me a seed. I miss all those pretty leaves, poor dears.

Rainy Day and School

The TV meteorologist so-called walks back and forth before the map,
But not outside of course, she'd muss her hair. Not like my dear teacher
Miss Tigner. She rode her bike through hail so she could tell us about its bite.
We sang the names of clouds, and she made fog and snow and rain, I don't
Know how. We acted parts—I was cirrus, my sister, cumulus. The twins
Got latitude and longitude. Bailey was lightning striking, Miss Tigner was God.

Today the weather channel's boring. I want to play, except I'm grown. I must
Be sick, or bad, I'm home alone. I pull on boots and go outside. The water runs
Off the roof and down my neck. I shake it off. Then, look out.
here come the ducks!
They're marching down Church Street. They're disobedient. I look both ways. The
Street's empty. I go out to the edge and sit on the garbage can and call the roll:

"Good morning, girls and boys," I clap my hands.
"Attention. Today the lesson is pre-cip-i-ta-tion."

Bob Dylan the Cat

Only a squeak escapes the cat's mouth, enough to make me turn
And ask what disturbs this soft compliant day. Dylan's talent
Is looking sweet in the eyes while sinking his teeth into a small
Gray furry disappearing thing. It happens each November: leaves
Blaze and fall, a cold comes on, no warning. Like wind-up toys,
Chipmunks scurry in random ways, then stop, played-out. I watch
With interest, nothing happens, we sit and wait—and what they're
Thinking, the chipmunks don't say.

The difference I bring to this one-way conversation is my aptitude for language.
I can make of Dylan's captive's squeak a testimony on a grand scale: survival of
The fittest, I say, and though Dylan's ahead for the moment, I know that I can say
What's going on from my lofty perch in my corner of my world. So to speak, I
Name the tune. I say what's up. I defy the odds. But must I have to think again
About the soft gray fur in Dylan's wet mouth, now lying gutted, its eyes squeezed
Shut, its little legs tucked up as if in sleep? I found it at the door. My gift for the day.

Dylan knows that I'm the first one out, the picker-up of leavings, the sorter-out
Of seasons, collecting rakes and coiling hoses, stonewalling against winter's teeth.
So it's understood I'm the one to get the pathetic thing, and I kick it off the porch,
And it's lost among the mottled leaves, though imprints a trace of blood on the porch.
I can handle it, Dylan. Look me in the eye, you hear me? I can handle anything you
Have to offer, except the squeak, so small, so helpless, so I don't know what.
I would have said so human, except not human, animal.

Fiction's Craft

A thin wisp of smoke rises
Off a quiet valley
And calls attention to
A scene in a house
At a moment when
Something is said
Between two people.

One turns away,
We cannot see the eyes.
The other's hand
Reaches for what?
Color the eyes hateful.
Bolt the door. What do
We care? What do we know?

Memory Floats

Porth Navas, Cornwall, England. The clang of riggings.
Arthur stands on the quay and studies the tide, turns
And hurries down the lane. Dahler has breakfast ready.
She's already been to the garden. They sit out,
Side by side, and drink their tea, sweeten their voices.

Next door, those noisy Americans, arrived late,
Slamming doors, losing keys, shouting over the village phone,
"We're here. It's just like the pictures. It's so quiet!"
The fox looked up, sniffed the air, and disappeared.
Finally, the Americans slept.

Now they all meet, talkative as can be. The post arrives noon.
The pub opens evenings. We wouldn't recommend the inn
Next town over. Such prices you wouldn't believe. We'd
Sooner eat at home ourselves. Go to St. Ives—it's free.

The Americans stay busy, busy, on-the-go. Then
Late at night, someone comes to an open window,
Looks far down the creek to the river to the sea.
Writes a message and tosses it in a bottle. Next

Morning, it's hard to tell the visitors from the natives,
So friendly are they all to sit in the sun, to drink their tea,
To read, or sleep, or walk in the lane, though no one knows
Of course what they really think, or where the sea goes.

Sudden Snow at the Colony

Artists go to sleep rich
And famous and
Wake up querulous.

Ginny revises the ending
Of her lousy novel.
Jeez, how many more
Times do we have to hear
About it. Pat shivers and
Draws a red hat to her spare
Self-portrait. Well, maybe.
David hates himself.
And why not.
Pages flame up in the grate
With Francine's wooden poems.
Good riddance. Me?
I'm the only one at work.

Meanwhile, the driver clears
Roads, the cook fries bacon,
And the day begins

The way the day begins:
On time, dependable,
And white, so surely white.

Winter's Tracks

Something not as big
As a polar bear
But more than a rabbit.
It couldn't hold a straight line
And stopped to shake snow
From the fir branches,
Then with nothing to lift up
Its own burden, it stumbled on,
In deeper tracks
Into the uncomplaining empty dark.

Subscription to Mother Nature

The look on the face
Of the downy red-tailed hawk
As she swallows whole
A newly hatched songbird
Is pure acceptance:

What father hawk brings
To the nest
She will eat

Even if the red legs
Thrash at her beak,
If readers turn a page
To pictures of bloody sunset.

The Accident

When a bird hit the windshield
No one had seen it coming.
What was that? A bird dead
On America's big highway,
Broken neck perhaps, don't
Look back.

So we rode on
In silence until sunset
Blinded us, and we stopped.
The child would not
Get out, his white face
Small against the glass,
His fingers tracing wings.

Journal Notes

When it begins, no one knows the end.
Snow carries its own weight,
Becoming deeper than our thoughts of it.

And nothing settles as in a permanence
Except memory. Though still we watch
The sky. What comes will be surprising

Like a friend who's unexpected
But as certain
As this brave December wind.

Poetic License

At first, you think it would be fine
To stretch out upon water,
To feel the length of your own body
Floating on the surface of things.

You think it would be better
To kick, make some motion,
Moving ahead with confidence,
Surprised by the ease.

The years pass, you know
Every motion, so certain,
So light you lift yourself
Out of your old body.

The moon races overhead,
You wait, you hold
Your breath, it's time:

You walk on water.

Cayuga Heights

Yes, I tell myself, a view, a thrill. Let yourself go.
Remember this, see that.
That's me, there   back from the edge.

Night's a deeper gorge. I draw blinds, set locks.
Blanketed, tossed and turned,
I wait for sleep, saying names,
Remember me. Sudden as wind
Banging the door, I wake to terror.
With my eyes I listen, my feet touch the floor.
I'm okay, I'm here, I've had a bad dream. The house
Sits on solid ground.

Distant as stars, the falls leap over and down
And nothing to
         hold on to
                 but broken sound.

Putting Fears to Rest

I've emptied out the coffee grounds and made some soup.
While it heats, I'll look out the window. The old neighbor's
Car's covered with snow. I wonder if she's dead.
What a terrible thing to say, but no one heard.
That's the awful part, there's no one to insult.

The soup's insulted, though. It's burned, the house filled
With smoke. I crack the door, the wind comes in, goes
Up the stairs, gets in the unmade bed, and moans.

The clock goes round and round and round until at last
The face lights up. It's nice to see another face beside
My own, which looks so tired. I try to sleep, give up
The ghost. What's that noise? Inside my chest,
A heart attack perhaps, but someone's at the door.

Come in, come in! Let's make more soup or love or
If you're staying long, let's sleep, my God, let's sleep.

The News of Spring

The wind scatters blossoms.
They fall and do not fly up
Again. In the wind's strength
The weak fall away.

Up high the trees
Put out a feathering
Of leaves. Clouds go on,
Passing a still afternoon.

In the ring of green
At the top of the sky,
Something's wrong: empty branches
Next to a splendor. The dead can
Do nothing

To help themselves but help
Others by giving up their place.
How long the old oak will require
To withdraw from the ring is
Known only in the root. How far it
Will fall and the great motion
Of air in the fall,

These are ways
We measure dying.

At the Fish Market

His name isn't important to me,
And I'd forget it,
But trying to remember
Last night's dream, that matters.

He knows my name, he thinks
He knows my politics,
He's seen me reading books,
And ain't that fancy?

I deny it is, without words,
Because words won't come
To me when he's explaining
What he'd do to flag-burners.

I stare at the shrimp.
He weighs it out, wraps it up,
And counts my change, still
In my face, now tight with fear.

How can this man with no name
Do it all at once, make change,
Conversation, stir up my hate,
When I'm just trying to remember

Last night's dream? I woke up,
Blinked, wondered where I was,
Saw it was my room, put on my
Glasses to see what floated by,

I remember all of that. It comes
Back and stops, but I know there's
Something more, someone I know
Who wants to tell me something,

But what? Please, please.
Get out of my life, mister,
Leave me alone.

Dudley's Twin Aunts

"We live in Rock Hill," Aunt Billie says, "but we bury in Birmingham."
"She's the smart one," Aunt Ella says, "and she won't deny it either."

All afternoon the guests arrive to stand in line, then, bending down,
Take the small, frail hands, lifted like Mama's pale handkerchiefs.

To be a twin is something marvelous, and now at 90, a surprise.
They smile and nod and look away, leaving a trace of memory

Like powdered sugar, dusting the cup's thin rim. Life's not been
Exactly a cup of tea for Dudley's twin aunts, and trouble hasn't always

Come in pairs. What's grief for one is different for another.
Their separate secrets are as mysterious as those blue, blue eyes—

The glance that darts between them like an arrow on the mark.

Carried over Water

Torrence Jennings wakes
To Aunt May's screams
And stumbles, running to put out the flames.
He's dreaming again, with no one to tell.
"I'm the last survivor on Portsmouth Island," he tells himself.

Daylight, he visits the graves,
Forgets what he came to say.

Voices carry over water.
Rust works the oar-locks,
Waves rise and fall.

All day he watches the clock:
It's time to meet the mail boat,
It's time to set the nets, to trim the wicks.
The day lengthens, and the sea rises.

Night after night the island moves toward shore.
Night after night Torrence Jennings takes a breath, and lets it go.

Seeking Permanence at Long Beach

October shadows measure loss:
The year erodes. Grasses sing
And are carried away. Piers
Fall into the sea.

Board up the windows,
Tie down the sun. Say farewell
To the wind, warning
Everything will be changed

When we come back again.

Waiting for the News

When the snow ceased blowing across the field
And doves ascended to tree branches, leaving
A whir of wings in an evening sky, silence hung

Over the house with a warning:
Do not say a word, do not breathe,
Let the moment pass over, be still.

There are some things you should walk away from

Not the young man ringing the bell for the Salvation Army—
Drop your coins in and his glad thanks will ring back.

Or an old aunt who stands shrunken at the door and calls,
"Come back to see me"—she will cost you so little.

But there are others to walk away from: learn who they are
So when they appear you'll have a ready answer:

Rich people who patronize the poor,
the self-righteous, the mean-spirited.
The duplicitous, the hypocritical.

Avoid discussing politics with bankers. And keep God to yourself.
Remember your old Grandmother's advice, and be happy.

Saying Goodbye

Never again will the phone ring on Sunday morning
"What'cha up to?"
"Not much. You?"
"Not much."
Then, all that silence, the pauses just before
Something breaks, and we try to pick up the pieces.

"I love you," you say
"I love you," I say
And nobody says,
Death is on the line.
Emily Dickinson understood,
We understand Emily Dickinson,
But it doesn't help.
Nothing helps.
Though you can quote more poetry
Than anyone who ever lived,
Or ever died,
Among my acquaintances.

Though you are more: you,
Linda, may I say your name,
Will it be okay? Am I taking away
Your only privilege, the privilege
Of privacy?
Your badge of honor,
So that when the doctor comes in,
He looks like a student,
And says it's time to do the tube,
You ask me to leave.

And I leave, grateful, as always
I have been grateful
For your gift: saying, Girl,
Go on now, girl.
Do what you have to do.
We'll be talking again.

Laurel Fork

Late frost on the apple blossoms:
deer do not come to the orchard
this autumn: this lean season.

At the End of a Season

All over the world,
But what do I know, really?
I was going to say, it's this way for everyone,
How we've come home tired, had a little something
To eat, maybe closed our eyes for a few minutes,
Said something to someone in a room, waited
For the response, nodded, not wanting to argue,
But knowing there was more work tomorrow,
That even if not in our house somewhere a child
With his eyes covered in flies and a big belly begs

Can't get it out of our minds   must be back
                                                          in some other time

I look out the window: there has been a nice rain,
After a hot day, and the lily is closed-up now, and
A small frog sits on the edge of a pond and faces
The night, that comes suddenly and frightens me still

Does it frighten you

With the ghost of a chance:

But tomorrow, we will begin again.

In Abiquiu, New Mexico
With Georgia O'Keeffe and Willa Cather

In an old adobe house, near the pueblo, on the edge of a hill, overlooking farmlands
A shadow lengthens and the weary world is hushed.
Along a passageway, through an open courtyard, into a room, out into the garden.
An old woman is asleep in the sun. Softly, walk softly, even the stones are sleeping.

In the bunkhouse on the high mesa under the stars above the lights of Ghost Ranch,
A lamp falls upon a page of an open book in the hands of a visitor far from home,
Who having flown fearfully above the clouds steadies her nerves for the millennium:
"Where there is great love there are always miracles." She reads & listens to the wind:

"One might almost say that an apparition is human vision corrected by divine love."
As overhead a star falls through the miraculous sky and lands on the open page, where
A woman reading, I am that woman, her "perceptions being made finer,"
Asks to see "what is there about us always" and discovers herself at home in the dark.

To Fly without Hurry

"Migrating birds passing lightships and lighthouses, or crossing the face
of the moon, have been observed to fly without hurry, or evidence
of straining to attain high speed."
        —The Migration of Birds, circular 15, Fish and Wildlife Service

Waking, we have gained an hour. What shall we do with it?
Where shall we go? Stay at home, don't answer the door.

Last night's moon threaded the hydrangea blossoms.
Let them dry paper-thin in tomorrow's sun.
The ghost at the foot of the bed, ask for her blessing.

The smoke that went up the chimney, let it go, and open a window
For the room to breathe. Oh, a little of this, a little of that, a nap,

A cup of tea, all appointments missed. Say farewell to the ladybug,
Welcome the doe to the meadow. Tonight we'll reach for the Big Dipper

And drink ourselves to sleep, counting the beat of wings.

History of a Small House

A house abandoned

I found a small house with a slanting porch
And an open door. I ran in like a mouse and made a nest.
And wrote my name on the wavy windowpane: Emly.
I could not spell but I could read.
I learned by heart the history of the house, but told no one.

Year after year in the city, I dreamed my sticks left in the yard
Burst into bloom. Last night, smoke rose from the chimney.

The birthplace

I don't know why I had not seen the place where I was born,
And when I asked to go, Daddy shook his head, "It's not the same."
Mama insisted she "never liked the place." I acted like a child and pouted.

Finally, he said he'd "sleep on it," and later I heard them arguing.
Morning, everything went wrong—I couldn't find the key,
The roads were wet and dangerous, the tires looked low. She said,

"I know the way, come on," and slammed the door. I followed
and said something funny and made her laugh. She let him
help her in the back seat, said I should sit up front to see.

"We could live here," he nodded to the passing countryside.
"Why, I'd be scared to death," she said. "I wouldn't stay alone."
I turned around and smiled and could not pretend to disagree.

Up the road we turned off to the town. The traffic lights he found
"ridiculous." She "wouldn't mind stopping" at the Antique Mall. We did.
A sugar bowl pleased. He winked, and the air lightened as after rain.

Then, wordless, he drove up a hill, took a wrong turn, turned back,
Then there it was: an empty house. "Rose Petal," he said, "Here's
Where you were born." "Someone's painted it blue," she frowned.

We wanted to get out, she didn't. He looked at me for help.
"Wait," she said. "We've come this far, I might as well go see."
"Oh look, my wintersweet is blooming!" We took her trembling hands.

The rented house

Under a thatched roof in a cottage in the Irish countryside, we
Were five, six with the lovely college girl, and I was the happy mother,
Taking care to warm the bottle, bake the bread, and stir the fire.
At night, I dropped coins in a meter to keep a hall light on.
Morning, I walked from the creamery with two frothy pitchers.
Rain or shine, we went, the professor at the wheel, to find the poets,
Towers, graveyards, and once a great house, windows opening to the sky,
Kept open for tours by an old coughing man. The house smelled dank.
Outside, I was afraid to look back, but did, and saw two old sisters
Sitting at a kitchen table, making tea. It was storybook, in most ways,
And though my bad time would come, I did not know it then, though
The baby whimpered in her sleep, said her first word, "Home."
"Soon, soon," I whispered, and listened for the meter ticking down.

My house

One afternoon after a long ride along the coast, I turned inward
And off the beaten track. The town was mostly gone. I was surprised
To find a small blue house, ragged robins blooming in the yard,
A homemade sign: For Sale. I said, Be mine. By night, I'd signed my name.

I put my favorite books on the shelves, a row of wooden houses on the mantel.
I set the table with a red cloth, a basket of lavender, and lighted candles.
I wrote long letters, sat in the swing. Last, I put a shell under my pillow.

Once I walked to the lighted phone booth in the closed-up town and turned back.
Fishing boats unloaded at the docks, singing their catch. I called across the water
And the water answered. I listened long. And so the summer passed, October

Came, and soon as a chill blew off the sound, I brought in wood and made a fire.
Then wrapping myself in Annie's quilt I lay down and went to sleep.
Someone stepped out of a picture frame and covered me up. I murmured thank you.

The distant gulls oared overhead. Sometime during the night,
It rained (the roof was tin). I thought it was a voice, calling my name.
Saying, you have found the words for longing, yours and mine.

52

Emily Herring Wilson writes poetry, essays, and women's history. She has been visiting writer for the North Carolina Arts Council and Cornell University and is a McDowell Fellow and a recipient of the Fortner Award from St. Andrews Presbyterian College. She lives in Winston-Salem, North Carolina.